The Complete Guide to Hemp Farming:

A Beginner's Handbook

There is growing evidence that exposure to plants and green spaces, especially gardening, benefits mental and physical health. You will discover a different world while growing cannabis.

Ali YILDIRIM

Published by Omega IP Holding, Inc.
Philadelphia, PA, United States
https://www.morzaik.us
ISBN: 978-1-970277-65-4
(Morzaik Publishing by Omega IP Holding, Inc)

Printed in the United States of America

Cover design & Illustrations by
Morzaik Publishing
First Edition – 2025

Table of Contents

Preface

For most of human history, hemp was simply a crop — as ordinary and essential as wheat or corn. Farmers grew it without controversy, weavers spun it into cloth, sailors relied on it for rope and sails, and healers used it for medicine. It was only in the twentieth century that hemp became entangled in political and legal battles that had little to do with the plant itself, effectively erasing centuries of agricultural knowledge from mainstream farming culture.

That knowledge is now coming back.

The legalization of commercial hemp cultivation in the United States under the 2018 Farm Bill marked a turning point — not just for American agriculture, but for the global conversation around sustainable farming. Suddenly, a crop with an extraordinary range of uses, a remarkably low environmental footprint, and genuine economic potential was available to farmers once again. The rush of interest that followed was understandable. So was the confusion.

Because here is the truth that many enthusiastic new hemp farmers discovered the hard way: growing hemp is not as simple as planting a seed and waiting for a profitable harvest. It is a crop that demands precision — in soil preparation, in seed selection, in water management, in pest control, and critically, in navigating a regulatory landscape that is still evolving. The margin for error is narrow, and the consequences of getting it wrong — a crop that tests hot for THC, a mold outbreak in the drying barn, a harvest with no buyer — can be financially devastating.

This handbook was written to close that gap between enthusiasm and preparation.

Whether you are a seasoned farmer considering adding hemp to your rotation, a landowner exploring new income streams, or someone entirely new to agriculture who has been drawn in by the promise of this remarkable plant, the pages that follow are designed to give you a realistic, practical, and honest foundation. You will find guidance on everything from selecting the right location and hemp variety for your goals, to managing your crop through the growing season, to processing your harvest and finding your place in the market.

Hemp farming rewards those who approach it with patience, curiosity, and a willingness to keep learning. This book is your starting point — not the final word, but a solid first step toward building a farming operation you can be proud of.

The field is waiting. Let's get to work.

Ali Yildirim

Chapter 1

Introduction to Hemp Farming

What is Hemp?

Hemp is a versatile and sustainable crop that has been grown for thousands of years for its various uses. It is a member of the Cannabis sativa plant species, but unlike its cousin marijuana, hemp contains very low levels of THC, the psychoactive compound that gives marijuana its intoxicating effects. This makes hemp non-intoxicating and safe for a wide range of uses.

Hemp has a long history of being used for industrial purposes, dating back to ancient civilizations. The fibers from the hemp plant are incredibly strong and durable, making them ideal for a variety of applications such as textiles, paper, and rope. Hemp seeds are also highly nutritious, containing high levels of protein, fiber, and essential fatty acids.

In recent years, hemp has gained popularity for its potential as a sustainable alternative to traditional crops. Hemp requires less water and pesticides to grow compared to crops like cotton, making it a more environmentally friendly option for farmers. Additionally, hemp plants have deep roots that help improve soil health and prevent erosion, making them a valuable crop for sustainable farming practices.

Hemp farming has seen a resurgence in the United States with the passage of the 2018 Farm Bill, which legalized the cultivation of hemp for commercial purposes. This has opened up new opportunities for farmers to diversify their crops and tap into the growing market for hemp-derived products such as CBD oil, textiles, and building materials. As more research is conducted on the potential uses of hemp, the industry is expected to continue to expand and innovate.

Overall, hemp is a valuable crop with a wide range of uses and benefits. Whether you are a farmer looking to diversify your crops, a consumer interested in sustainable products, or someone curious about the potential of hemp, there is a lot to learn and explore in the world of hemp farming. With its long history and promising future, hemp is a crop that is sure to continue making an impact in various industries for years to come.

History of Hemp Farming

Hemp has been cultivated for thousands of years, with its history dating back to ancient civilizations such as the Chinese, Egyptians, and Mesopotamians. These early civilizations used hemp for a variety of purposes, including fiber for textiles, food, and medicinal applications. Hemp farming has a rich and diverse history that spans across continents and cultures.

In ancient China, hemp was considered one of the "five grains," along with rice, wheat, barley, and soybeans. It was used to make paper, fabric, and rope, as well as for medicinal purposes. The Chinese also discovered the psychoactive properties of the plant and used it for spiritual and recreational purposes.

In ancient Egypt, hemp was used to make ropes, sails, and textiles. The Egyptians also used hemp seeds for food and oil. Hemp was so valuable in ancient Egypt that it was sometimes used as a form of currency. The plant was also used in religious ceremonies and rituals.

In Europe, hemp farming became widespread during the Middle Ages. European countries such as France, Spain, and Italy cultivated hemp for its fiber, which was used to make clothing, sails, and ropes for ships. Hemp was an essential crop for many European economies, and it was often grown by peasants and farmers as a cash crop. In the United States, hemp farming was prevalent in the early colonial period. The plant was grown by farmers such as George Washington and Thomas Jefferson, who both advocated for its cultivation. Hemp was used to make paper, textiles, and rope in the early American colonies. However, hemp farming declined in the 20th century due to changing regulations and attitudes towards the plant. Today, hemp farming is experiencing a resurgence as more people recognize

the plant's potential for sustainable agriculture and economic growth.

Benefits of Hemp Farming

Hemp farming is becoming increasingly popular due to the numerous benefits it offers to farmers and the environment. One of the key benefits of hemp farming is its sustainability. Hemp plants require minimal water and can grow in a variety of soil types, making them a versatile crop that can thrive in different environments. Unlike many other crops, hemp also has a short growing cycle, typically ranging from 70 to 140 days, which means farmers can harvest multiple crops in a single year.

In addition to being a sustainable crop, hemp farming is also beneficial for the environment. Hemp plants have deep roots that help to prevent soil erosion and improve soil health. They can also absorb high levels of carbon dioxide from the atmosphere, making them an effective tool for combating climate change. Furthermore, hemp plants are naturally resistant to pests, reducing the need for harmful pesticides that can harm the environment and human health.

Another significant benefit of hemp farming is its versatility. Hemp plants can be used to produce a wide range of products, including textiles, paper, building materials, and biofuels. The seeds of the hemp plant are also rich in nutrients and can be used to produce hemp oil, which is high in omega-3 and omega-6 fatty acids. This versatility makes hemp farming a lucrative option for farmers looking to diversify their crops and explore new markets.

Moreover, hemp farming can also provide economic benefits to farmers. The demand for hemp products is growing rapidly, creating new opportunities for farmers to capitalize on this emerging market. In addition, hemp cultivation can help to revitalize rural communities by providing new sources of income and employment. By investing in hemp farming, farmers can not only improve their own livelihoods but also contribute to the growth of a sustainable and environmentally friendly industry.

Overall, hemp farming offers a multitude of benefits to farmers, the environment, and the economy. As more people become aware of the advantages of hemp cultivation, it is likely that the industry will continue to expand and thrive. Whether you are a seasoned farmer looking to diversify your crops or a newcomer interested in sustainable agriculture, hemp farming is definitely worth considering as a viable and rewarding option.

Chapter 2

Getting Started with Hemp Farming

Legalities of Hemp Farming

Dealing with hemp regulations is less about reading the fine print and more about protecting your entire financial investment. Unlike traditional crops, hemp is heavily monitored because of its genetic relationship to marijuana. If your crop tests even a fraction of a percent over the legal 0.3% THC limit, it is considered "hot." In many jurisdictions, a hot crop must be completely destroyed by law enforcement or state agricultural departments, resulting in a total loss for the farmer. Therefore, testing your plants early and often isn't just a regulatory hoop to jump through; it is the ultimate insurance policy for your farm.

While both plants come from the cannabis family, hemp contains very low levels of THC, the psychoactive compound found in marijuana. In the

United States, the 2018 Farm Bill legalized the cultivation of hemp as long as it contains no more than 0.3% THC on a dry weight basis. Understanding this distinction is essential for hemp farmers to ensure they are growing a legal crop.

Another important legal consideration for hemp farmers is licensing. In many states and countries, farmers are required to obtain a license to grow hemp. These licenses often come with specific requirements and regulations that must be followed, such as testing for THC levels and keeping detailed records of cultivation practices. Failure to comply with these licensing requirements can result in fines or even criminal charges.

In addition to licensing, hemp farmers must also be aware of regulations surrounding the sale and distribution of hemp products. This includes guidelines for labeling, testing, and marketing hemp products. It is important for farmers to stay up to date on these regulations to ensure they are producing and selling their products legally.

Overall, understanding the legalities of hemp farming is essential for anyone involved in this industry. By staying informed and compliant with regulations, hemp farmers can ensure the success and longevity of their operations. It is recommended that farmers consult with legal professionals or industry experts to navigate the complex legal landscape of hemp farming.

Choosing the Right Location

You can buy the best genetics in the world, but if your field sits in a low-lying frost pocket or heavy clay that pools water after a storm, your season will be an uphill battle. Hemp absolutely despises "wet feet." If the root zone remains flooded for even a few days, the plants will stunt and become highly susceptible to root rot. When scouting a location, look for gentle slopes that offer natural water runoff, and pay attention to historical frost dates in that specific microclimate.

One of the most important factors to consider when choosing a location for your hemp farm is the climate. Hemp plants thrive in warm, humid environments with plenty of sunlight. It is important to select a location that receives at least 8 10 hours of sunlight per day and has a consistent temperature range of 60 80 degrees Fahrenheit.

Additionally, hemp plants require a certain amount of rainfall to grow properly, so be sure to consider the average precipitation levels in your chosen location.

Another key factor to consider when choosing a location for your hemp farm is soil quality. Hemp plants require well- drained soil with a pH level between 6.0 and 7.5. It is also important to select a location with nutrient-rich soil that is free from contaminants such as heavy metals or pesticides. Conducting a soil test before planting your hemp crop can help you determine if the soil in your chosen location is suitable for growing hemp.

In addition to climate and soil quality, it is important to consider local regulations when choosing a location for your hemp farm. Some areas have strict regulations regarding the cultivation of hemp, including licensing requirements and zoning restrictions. Be sure to research the laws and regulations in your area before selecting a location for your hemp farm to ensure that you are in compliance with all applicable rules.

Overall, choosing the right location for your hemp farm is essential for the success of your operation. By considering factors such as climate, soil quality, and local regulations, you can maximize your chances of a successful harvest. Take the time to research potential locations thoroughly and consult with experts in the field to ensure that you are making the best choice for your hemp farm.

Selecting Hemp Varieties

Buying hemp seeds isn't like buying corn or soybeans. Your seed genetics dictate your entire business model. Before you even look at a seed catalog, you need to know exactly who is buying your harvest. Processors looking for CBD isolate require entirely different plant profiles than manufacturers buying stalks for industrial textiles. If you plant a fiber variety but hope to sell it to a CBD extractor, your crop will be practically worthless. Start by locking in your end-buyer, figure out exactly what cannabinoid profile or fiber length they require, and work backward to choose your seed.

When selecting hemp varieties, it is important to first consider the end products you hope to produce. Different varieties of hemp are bred for specific purposes, such as fiber production, seed production, or cannabinoid extraction. If you are interested in producing CBD or other cannabinoids, you will want to choose a high-CBD strain. On the other hand, if you are looking to produce hemp for fiber or seed, you will need to select a variety that is suited for those purposes.

Another important factor to consider when selecting hemp varieties is the growing conditions in your region. Hemp is a versatile crop that can thrive in a wide range of climates and soil types, but certain varieties may perform better in specific conditions. Consider factors such as temperature, rainfall, and soil quality when choosing a hemp variety to ensure optimal growth and yield.

In addition to considering end products and growing conditions, it is important to be aware of regulations surrounding hemp cultivation. In many regions, hemp farming is subject to strict regulations regarding THC content, licensing, and testing. Make sure to research the regulations in your area and choose hemp varieties that comply with local laws to avoid potential legal issues and ensure a successful harvest.

Overall, selecting the right hemp varieties is a crucial step in the success of your hemp farming operation. By considering factors such as desired end products, growing conditions, and regulations, you can choose varieties that are well-suited to your specific needs and increase the likelihood of a profitable harvest. Remember to do thorough research and seek advice from experienced farmers or hemp experts to make informed decisions when selecting hemp varieties for your farm.

Chapter 3

Soil Preparation and Planting

Soil Testing and Analysis

Guessing your soil's nutrient profile is the fastest way to burn through your farming budget. Hemp is an incredibly aggressive bioaccumulator, meaning it pulls heavy metals, toxins, and nutrients out of the earth at a rapid pace. Before a single seed goes into the ground, a comprehensive lab analysis of your soil is mandatory. You aren't just looking at standard N-P-K (Nitrogen, Phosphorus, Potassium) levels; you need to verify that your soil is free of residual pesticides and heavy metals from previous decades of farming, which can easily contaminate a modern CBD harvest.

The first step in soil testing and analysis is to collect soil samples from various locations on your farm. This will give you a comprehensive picture of the overall health and composition of your soil. You can either do this yourself using a soil probe or hire a professional soil testing service to collect and analyze the samples for you. Once you have your soil samples, you can send them off to a laboratory for testing. The results will provide you with valuable information about the nutrient levels, pH balance, and other important factors that will influence the success of your hemp crop.

One of the key benefits of soil testing and analysis is the ability to tailor your fertilizer and nutrient management plan to the specific needs of your soil. By knowing which nutrients are lacking or in excess, you can make targeted adjustments to ensure your hemp plants have everything they need to thrive. This can help you avoid over-fertilizing, which can lead to nutrient runoff and environmental pollution, as well as under-fertilizing, which can result in stunted growth and low yields.

In addition to nutrient management, soil testing and analysis can also help you determine the best varieties of hemp to plant on your farm. Different hemp varieties have different nutrient requirements and tolerances to various soil conditions. By understanding your soil composition, you can choose varieties that are well-suited to your specific growing conditions, resulting in healthier plants and higher yields. This targeted approach can help you maximize the potential of your hemp farm and achieve greater success in your farming endeavors.

In conclusion, soil testing and analysis are essential tools for any hemp farmer looking to optimize their crop yield and quality. By understanding the composition of your soil, you can make informed decisions about nutrient management, pH adjustment, and variety selection. Investing in soil testing and analysis can help you avoid costly mistakes, improve the health of your soil, and ultimately increase the success of your hemp farming operation. By taking the time to understand and optimize your soil, you can set yourself up for a successful and sustainable hemp farming future.

Soil Amendments for Hemp Cultivation

Soil amendments play a crucial role in the success of hemp cultivation. By enriching the soil with the right nutrients and minerals, farmers can ensure healthy plant growth and higher yields. In this section, we will discuss the various soil amendments that are beneficial for hemp farming.

One of the most common soil amendments for hemp cultivation is compost. Compost is a nutrient-rich organic material that helps improve soil structure, fertility, and water retention. By adding compost to the soil, farmers can provide essential nutrients to the hemp plants and promote healthy root development. Compost also helps to increase microbial activity in the soil, which is essential for nutrient uptake by the plants.

Another important soil amendment for hemp cultivation is biochar. Biochar is a type of charcoal that is produced by burning organic material in a low-oxygen environment.

When added to the soil, biochar helps improve soil structure, water retention, and nutrient retention. It also acts as a carbon sink, helping to reduce greenhouse gas emissions. By incorporating biochar into their soil, farmers can improve the overall health and productivity of their hemp crops.

In addition to compost and biochar, farmers can also use organic fertilizers as soil amendments for hemp cultivation. Organic fertilizers, such as manure, bone meal, and fish emulsion, provide essential nutrients to the soil and promote healthy plant growth. Unlike synthetic fertilizers, organic fertilizers release nutrients slowly over time, reducing the risk of nutrient runoff and pollution. By using organic fertilizers, farmers can ensure that their hemp crops are healthy and free from harmful chemicals.

It is important for farmers to test their soil regularly to determine which soil amendments are needed for optimal hemp cultivation. By conducting soil tests, farmers can identify any nutrient deficiencies or imbalances in the soil and make informed decisions about which soil amendments to use. By choosing the right soil amendments and maintaining healthy soil, farmers can ensure successful hemp cultivation and achieve higher yields.

Planting Techniques for Hemp

Planting hemp requires careful consideration and planning to ensure a successful crop. In this subchapter, we will discuss some essential planting techniques for hemp that every farmer should be familiar with. By following these guidelines, you can optimize your hemp farm's productivity and yield.

One of the most critical aspects of planting hemp is selecting the right location. Hemp thrives in well-drained soil with good fertility and adequate sunlight. It is essential to choose a site that receives at least 6

8 hours of direct sunlight per day. Additionally, hemp plants are sensitive to water-logged conditions, so make sure to avoid planting in areas prone to flooding or poor drainage.

When it comes to planting hemp seeds, proper spacing is key. Hemp plants require ample space to grow and develop, so be sure to plant your seeds at least 6 8 inches apart in rows that are 4 6 feet apart. This will allow each plant to have enough room to spread out and receive adequate sunlight and nutrients. Additionally, planting in rows will make it easier to manage weeds and pests throughout the growing season.

It is also essential to consider the timing of planting hemp seeds. Hemp is a warm-season crop that thrives in temperatures between 60 80 degrees Fahrenheit. Ideally, seeds should be planted in early to mid-spring once the soil has warmed up and there is no longer a risk of frost. Planting too early can result in poor germination rates, while planting too late can lead to reduced yields.

Finally, it is crucial to properly prepare the soil before planting hemp seeds. This includes testing the soil pH and nutrient levels and making any necessary amendments to ensure optimal growing conditions. Additionally, consider using cover crops or green manure to improve soil structure and fertility. By following these planting techniques for hemp, you can set your farm up for success and maximize your hemp crop's potential.

Chapter 4

Hemp Crop Management

Watering and Irrigation Systems

Hemp is notoriously thirsty during its vegetative state, rapidly consuming water to fuel its explosive vertical growth. However, this high water demand is a delicate balancing act. While the canopy needs moisture to expand, the root system requires oxygen. Relying solely on rainfall is a massive gamble, which is why precision irrigation is usually required for commercial success. Setting up a localized delivery system allows you to control the exact volume of water reaching the root zone, reducing evaporation and preventing the soil from becoming a waterlogged breeding ground for disease.

One common method of watering hemp plants is through the use of drip irrigation systems. Drip irrigation delivers water directly to the base of the plant through a network of tubes and emitters. This method is efficient in delivering water where it is needed most, reducing water waste and minimizing the risk of overwatering. Drip irrigation systems can be easily customized to suit the specific needs of a hemp farm, making them a popular choice among hemp farmers.

Another popular irrigation system for hemp farming is overhead sprinklers. These systems deliver water through a series of sprinkler heads that distribute water evenly over the entire crop. Overhead sprinklers are ideal for larger hemp farms, as they can cover a wide area with minimal effort. However, it is important to monitor the moisture levels of the soil to prevent overwatering and ensure the health of the plants.

In addition to traditional irrigation systems, hemp farmers may also consider utilizing rainwater harvesting techniques. Rainwater harvesting involves collecting and storing rainwater for later use in irrigation. This sustainable practice can help reduce water costs and reliance on traditional water sources. By capturing and storing rainwater, hemp farmers can ensure a consistent water supply for their crops, even during periods of drought.

Overall, choosing the right watering and irrigation system is crucial for the success of a hemp farm. Whether utilizing drip irrigation, overhead sprinklers, or rainwater harvesting techniques, it is important to monitor soil moisture levels and adjust watering practices accordingly. By implementing efficient watering and irrigation systems, hemp farmers can promote healthy plant growth, maximize yield, and contribute to the overall success of their farm.

Pest and Disease Control

Because hemp is often grown for human consumption—especially in the CBD and seed oil markets—traditional chemical pesticides are usually completely off the table. A crop sprayed with unapproved chemicals will fail laboratory testing and be rejected by buyers. This means farmers must rely heavily on Integrated Pest Management (IPM). Instead of reaching for a chemical spray when you see aphids or russet mites, you have to create an ecosystem that fights back. This involves releasing predatory insects like ladybugs, introducing beneficial nematodes into the soil, and actively walking your rows every single day to catch infestations before they spread.

One of the most common pests that hemp farmers encounter is the hemp borer. These insects feed on the stems and leaves of hemp plants, causing significant damage. To control hemp borers, it is essential to regularly inspect plants for signs of infestation and take proactive measures to prevent their spread. This may include the use of insecticidal sprays or the introduction of natural predators to the growing environment. Another common pest that hemp farmers must contend with is the hemp russet mite.

These tiny pests feed on the sap of hemp plants, causing leaves to curl and turn yellow. To control hemp russet mites, growers can use insecticidal soaps or neem oil sprays. It is also important to maintain proper humidity levels in the growing environment, as these mites thrive in dry conditions.

In addition to pests, hemp plants are also susceptible to a variety of diseases, such as powdery mildew and root rot. Powdery mildew presents as a white powdery substance on the leaves of hemp plants, while root rot causes the roots to become soft and mushy. To prevent these diseases, growers should practice proper sanitation techniques, such as removing infected plants and debris from the growing area. Overall, pest and disease control is a critical aspect of successful hemp farming. By staying vigilant and implementing proactive measures to prevent infestations, growers can protect their crops and ensure a healthy harvest. Additionally, proper crop rotation and soil management practices can help reduce the risk of pests and diseases, leading to higher yields and better quality hemp products.

Weed Management in Hemp Fields

Weed management is a crucial aspect of maintaining  a successful hemp farm. Weeds can compete with hemp plants for nutrients, sunlight, and water, ultimately reducing the yield and quality of the crop. It is essential for hemp farmers to implement effective weed management strategies to ensure the health and productivity of their fields.

There are several methods that can be used to control weeds in hemp fields. One common approach is mechanical cultivation, which involves using tools such as cultivators or hoes to physically remove weeds from the soil. This method is effective for small-scale operations but may be labor-intensive and time- consuming for larger farms.

Another popular weed management technique in hemp farming is the use of mulch. Mulching involves covering the soil around hemp plants with materials such as straw, wood chips, or plastic to suppress weed growth. Mulching not only helps to control weeds but also conserves moisture in the soil and improves soil health.

Chemical herbicides can also be used to control weeds in hemp fields, but it is essential to use them responsibly and in accordance with local regulations. Organic herbicides derived from natural sources such as vinegar or essential oils can be effective alternatives to synthetic chemicals.

In conclusion, weed management is a critical aspect of hemp farming that requires careful planning and implementation. By using a combination of mechanical cultivation, mulching, and responsible herbicide use, hemp farmers can effectively control weeds and promote the health and productivity of their fields. It is essential for all hemp farmers to prioritize weed management to ensure the success of their crops and the sustainability of their operations.

Chapter 5

Harvesting and Processing Hemp

Harvesting Hemp Plants

The harvest window for hemp is notoriously tight, often forcing farmers to make high-stakes decisions based on the daily weather forecast. Wait too long to harvest a cannabinoid crop, and your THC levels might spike past legal limits, or an early autumn frost could damage the flowers. Cut too early, and you leave valuable CBD weight in the field. Having a solid labor plan and the right machinery on standby *before* the trichomes turn amber is the only way to ensure you don't lose your crop to the calendar.

When harvesting hemp plants, it is important to use the proper tools and techniques to ensure a successful harvest. Many farmers opt to use a combine harvester or a sickle bar mower to efficiently cut down the plants. It is important to cut the plants close to the ground to ensure that as much of the valuable biomass is captured. Once the plants have been cut, they are typically left in the field to dry for a few days before being transported to a drying facility.

After the hemp plants have been harvested and dried, the next step is to extract the valuable compounds from the plant material. This is typically done using a process called decortication, which involves separating the fibers, seeds, and flowers from the stalk of the plant. The extracted fibers can be used for a variety of industrial purposes, while the seeds can be processed for their oil content. The flowers, which contain high levels of cannabinoids like CBD, can be used for medicinal or recreational purposes.

Harvesting hemp plants can be a labor-intensive process, but the rewards are well worth the effort.

By following proper harvesting techniques and using the right tools, farmers can ensure a successful harvest that yields high-quality hemp biomass. With the growing demand for hemp products in various industries, mastering the art of harvesting hemp plants is essential for any aspiring hemp farmer.

In conclusion, harvesting hemp plants is a crucial step in the hemp farming process that requires careful timing, proper tools, and techniques. By understanding when to harvest, how to cut the plants, and how to extract the valuable compounds, farmers can maximize the potential of their hemp crop. With the right knowledge and skills, anyone can successfully harvest hemp plants and contribute to the thriving hemp industry.

Drying and Curing Hemp

You can grow a flawless, beautiful crop in the field, but if you rush the drying phase, you can ruin it in a matter of days. Throwing wet hemp into a hot, unventilated barn is a recipe for catastrophic mold outbreaks. The goal isn't to dry the plant as fast as possible; the goal is to carefully draw the moisture out while preserving the fragile terpenes and cannabinoids. Investing in commercial dehumidifiers, industrial fans, and proper hanging racks pays for itself the moment you prevent a mold spore from wiping out a year's worth of work.

The first step in drying hemp is to harvest the plants when they have reached the optimal maturity level. This is typically indicated by the plants' trichomes turning from a milky white color to an amber hue.

Once harvested, the plants should be hung in a well-ventilated area with good airflow to prevent mold and mildew growth. It is important to monitor the humidity levels in the drying area to ensure that they remain between 45 55% for optimal drying conditions.

Curing hemp involves storing the dried plants in a cool, dark, and dry environment for an extended period of time. This process allows the cannabinoids and terpenes in the plant to further develop, resulting in a smoother and more flavorful end product. Curing can take anywhere from a few weeks to a few months, depending on the desired outcome. It is important to regularly check on the plants during the curing process to ensure that they are properly drying out and not developing mold.

Properly dried and cured hemp should have a moisture content of around 10 15%. This can be achieved by using a moisture meter to regularly monitor the plants' moisture levels. Over-drying the hemp can result in a harsh and unpleasant smoking experience, while under-drying can lead to mold growth and a loss of potency. By following these guidelines for drying and curing hemp, you can produce a high-quality product that meets industry standards and satisfies consumer demand.

In conclusion, drying and curing hemp are essential steps in the cultivation process that can greatly impact the quality and market value of the final product. By following best practices for drying and curing, you can produce a premium product that meets industry standards and satisfies consumer demand.

Remember to harvest your plants at the optimal maturity level, dry them in a well- ventilated area with good airflow, and cure them in a cool, dark, and dry environment. By monitoring humidity levels, moisture content, and regularly checking on the plants during the curing process, you can ensure that your hemp is properly dried and cured for the best possible results.

Processing hemp for various end uses is a crucial step in maximizing the potential of this versatile crop. Hemp can be used for a wide range of products, from textiles and paper to food and biofuels. Understanding the different processing methods available can help farmers make informed decisions about how to best utilize their hemp harvest.

One common method of processing hemp is decortication, which involves separating the fibers from the woody inner core of the plant, known as the hurd. Decorticated hemp fibers can be used to make textiles, ropes, and paper products. This process requires specialized equipment, such as a decortication machine, to efficiently separate the fibers from the hurd.

Another important processing method for hemp is extraction, which involves extracting the beneficial compounds, such as CBD, from the plant material. This can be done using various methods, including solvent extraction, CO_2 extraction, and ethanol extraction.

The extracted compounds can then be used to make a wide range of products, including CBD oil, tinctures, and topicals.

In addition to decortication and extraction, hemp can also be processed for food and biofuel production. Hemp seeds are a nutritious source of protein, omega-3 fatty acids, and other essential nutrients. They can be used to make hemp oil, protein powder, and other food products. Hemp can also be used to produce biofuels, such as biodiesel, which can help reduce our reliance on fossil fuels.

Overall, processing hemp for various end uses is an essential part of maximizing the potential of this valuable crop. By understanding the different processing methods available, farmers can make informed decisions about how to best utilize their hemp harvest. Whether it's for textiles, CBD products, food, or biofuels, hemp has the potential to revolutionize multiple industries and provide sustainable solutions for a wide range of applications.

Chapter 6

Marketing and Selling Hemp Products

Understanding the Hemp Market

Understanding the hemp market is essential for anyone involved in the hemp farming industry. With the recent legalization of hemp in many countries, including the United States, the market for hemp products is booming. Hemp is a versatile crop that can be used for a wide range of products, including textiles, paper, biofuels, and even food and medicine. By understanding the ins and outs of the hemp market, farmers can position themselves for success in this rapidly growing industry.

One key aspect of understanding the hemp market is knowing the different sectors within the industry. Hemp can be divided into three main categories: industrial hemp, medical hemp, and CBD hemp. Industrial hemp is used for its fibers and seeds, which can be used to make a variety of products such as textiles, paper, and biofuels. Medical hemp refers to hemp plants that are high in CBD, a non-psychoactive compound that has been shown to have numerous health benefits. CBD hemp is used to produce CBD products such as oils, tinctures, and edibles.

Another important factor to consider when understanding the hemp market is the legal landscape surrounding hemp production and sales. While hemp is now legal in many countries, including the United States, there are still regulations and restrictions that farmers must adhere to. For example, in the US, hemp farmers must obtain a license from the Department of Agriculture and adhere to strict guidelines regarding THC levels in their crops. Understanding these regulations is crucial for ensuring compliance and avoiding any legal issues.

Market trends and consumer preferences are also important factors to consider when understanding the hemp market. As the demand for sustainable and eco-friendly products continues to grow, hemp is becoming increasingly popular among consumers. In addition, the growing awareness of the health benefits of CBD has led to a surge in demand for CBD products. By staying informed about market trends and consumer preferences, hemp farmers can better position themselves to meet the needs of their target market and maximize their profits.

In conclusion, understanding the hemp market is crucial for anyone involved in the hemp farming industry. By knowing the different sectors within the industry, staying informed about regulations and legal requirements, and keeping up-to-date on market trends and consumer preferences, farmers can position themselves for success in this rapidly growing industry. With the right knowledge and strategies in place, hemp farmers can take advantage of the booming hemp market and achieve long-term success in this exciting and lucrative industry.

Creating a Brand for Your Hemp Products

The modern hemp market is absolutely flooded with generic green leaves and standard wellness jargon. To stand out on a retail shelf or in an online store, your brand needs a highly specific identity. Are you targeting athletes looking for muscle recovery? Are you positioning your hemp seed oil as a gourmet culinary ingredient? Your packaging, your website copy, and your photography all need to speak directly to that specific demographic. If you try to market your product to everyone, you will end up appealing to no one.

One of the first steps in creating a brand for your hemp products is to develop a unique selling proposition USP . This is what sets your products apart from the competition and gives customers a reason to choose your brand. Your USP could be anything from the quality of your hemp products to your commitment to sustainability and ethical sourcing.

Once you have established your USP, it is important to create a visual identity for your brand. This includes designing a logo, choosing a color scheme, and creating packaging that reflects the values of your company. Your visual identity should be consistent across all of your marketing materials and products to create a cohesive brand image.

In addition to a strong visual identity, it is important to have a clear brand message that resonates with your target audience. This message should communicate the benefits of your hemp products and why customers should choose your brand over others. Whether it is promoting the health benefits of hemp or emphasizing your commitment to organic farming practices, your brand message should be authentic and compelling.

Finally, building a brand for your hemp products also involves creating a strong online presence. This includes having a professional website, engaging with customers on social media, and utilizing digital marketing strategies to reach a wider audience. By effectively communicating your brand values and benefits online, you can attract new customers and build loyalty among existing ones.

Selling Hemp Products Online and Offline

Selling hemp products, both online and offline, can be a lucrative business opportunity for hemp farmers. By tapping into the growing demand for hemp-based products, farmers can expand their customer base and increase their revenue streams. In this subchapter, we will explore the ins and outs of selling hemp products in both online and offline markets.

One of the key advantages of selling hemp products online is the ability to reach a larger audience. With the rise of e-commerce platforms, farmers can easily set up online stores to showcase their products to customers around the world. This allows farmers to tap into a global market and connect with consumers who are looking for high-quality hemp products. Additionally, online selling can be more cost-effective than traditional brick-and-mortar stores, as it eliminates the need for physical storefronts and reduces overhead expenses.

When selling hemp products online, farmers should focus on creating a strong brand presence and leveraging digital marketing strategies to attract customers. This includes optimizing their website for search engines, engaging with customers on social media, and utilizing email marketing campaigns to promote their products. By building a strong online presence, farmers can establish themselves as trusted providers of high-quality hemp products and attract a loyal customer base.

In addition to selling hemp products online, farmers can also explore offline sales channels to reach local customers. This can include selling products at farmers markets, craft fairs, and specialty stores in their area. By participating in local events and establishing relationships with retailers, farmers can increase their visibility and attract customers who prefer to shop in person. Offline sales can also provide opportunities for farmers to educate consumers about the benefits of hemp products and build personal connections with their customers.

Overall, selling hemp products online and offline can be a rewarding endeavor for hemp farmers looking to expand their business. By leveraging the power of e-commerce platforms and exploring offline sales channels, farmers can reach a wider audience, increase their revenue streams, and establish themselves as trusted providers of high- quality hemp products. With the right strategies and marketing tactics, farmers can successfully grow their hemp business and contribute to the growing popularity of hemp products in the market.

Chapter 7

Challenges and Opportunities in Hemp Farming

Common Challenges Faced by Hemp Farmers

Farming hemp isn't just about battling aphids and unpredictable rain; it is about surviving a wildly fluctuating market. When the Farm Bill first passed, a "green rush" mentality flooded the market with raw biomass, causing prices to crash and leaving many farmers with barns full of unsold crops. The modern hemp farmer has to be just as skilled at reading market reports and negotiating processing contracts as they are at driving a tractor. Securing a buyer before you even buy your seeds is the safest way to insulate yourself from sudden price drops.

One of the most significant challenges faced by hemp farmers is the lack of clear regulations and guidelines surrounding the cultivation of hemp. As hemp is a relatively new crop in many regions, farmers often find themselves navigating a complex web of regulations that can vary from state to state or country to country. This lack of clarity can make it difficult for farmers to understand what is expected of them and can lead to confusion and frustration.

Another common challenge faced by hemp farmers is the issue of seed sourcing. Finding high-quality hemp seeds that are suited to their specific growing conditions can be a daunting task for many farmers. Additionally, the cost of purchasing certified hemp seeds can be prohibitive for some farmers, leading them to consider using lower-quality seeds that may not yield the desired results.

Pest and disease management is another challenge that hemp farmers must contend with. Hemp is susceptible to a variety of pests and diseases, and without proper management practices in place, farmers risk losing their entire crop to infestations or infections. Developing a comprehensive pest and disease management plan is essential for hemp farmers to protect their crops and ensure a successful harvest.

Weather fluctuations and environmental factors can also pose challenges for hemp farmers. Hemp is a sensitive crop that requires specific growing conditions to thrive, and unexpected weather events such as droughts, floods, or extreme temperatures can have a significant impact on crop yields. Farmers must be prepared to adapt to changing weather patterns and implement strategies to mitigate the effects of unfavorable conditions on their crops.

Finally, marketing and distribution can present challenges for hemp farmers, as the market for hemp products can be volatile and competitive. Developing a marketing strategy to promote their products and establish relationships with buyers can be a daunting task for many farmers, especially those who are new to the industry. By understanding and addressing these common challenges, hemp farmers can increase their chances of success and build a sustainable and profitable hemp farming business.

Emerging opportunities in the Hemp Industry

As the hemp industry continues to grow and evolve, new opportunities are emerging for farmers and entrepreneurs alike. In this subchapter, we will explore some of the most exciting trends and developments in the world of hemp farming, and how you can take advantage of them to build a successful business in this booming industry.

One of the most exciting emerging opportunities in the hemp industry is the increasing demand for hemp-based products. From CBD oils and tinctures to hemp textiles and building materials, consumers are increasingly turning to hemp for its many benefits.

This growing demand presents a unique opportunity for farmers to capitalize on the popularity of hemp and diversify their operations to meet this demand. Another emerging opportunity in the hemp industry is the development of new technologies and techniques for growing and processing hemp.

Advances in genetics, cultivation methods, and extraction processes are making it easier and more cost-effective to produce high-quality hemp products. By staying up to date on the latest innovations in the industry, farmers can position themselves as leaders in the field and continue to grow their businesses.

In addition to new product opportunities and technological advancements, there are also emerging opportunities in the international hemp market. As more countries legalize hemp cultivation and trade barriers are reduced, the global market for hemp products is expanding rapidly. This presents a unique opportunity for farmers to tap into new markets and reach customers around the world, helping to further grow and diversify their businesses.

Overall, the hemp industry is full of exciting opportunities for farmers and entrepreneurs looking to enter this rapidly growing market. By staying informed about the latest trends and developments, and by being willing to adapt and innovate, you can position yourself for success in this dynamic and evolving industry.

Whether you are a seasoned farmer looking to diversify your operations or a newcomer interested in starting a hemp farm, now is the perfect time to get involved in this exciting and profitable industry.

Sustainable Practices in Hemp Farming

In recent years, sustainable practices in hemp farming have become increasingly important as the demand for hemp products continues to rise. As more and more people turn to hemp for its versatile uses in textiles, paper, food, and more, it is crucial that we prioritize environmentally- friendly methods of cultivation.

Sustainable hemp farming not only benefits the planet by reducing carbon emissions and preserving natural resources, but it also ensures the longevity and success of the hemp industry for future generations.

One of the key principles of sustainable hemp farming is organic cultivation. By avoiding the use of synthetic pesticides, herbicides, and fertilizers, organic hemp farmers can protect the health of the soil, water, and surrounding ecosystems. Organic farming practices also help to maintain the biodiversity of the farm, promoting a healthy balance of insects, plants, and microbes that support the overall health of the hemp crop. Additionally, organic hemp is often of higher quality and can command a premium price in the market.

Another important aspect of sustainable hemp farming is water conservation. Hemp is a water-intensive crop, requiring significant amounts of water to grow and thrive.

By implementing water-saving techniques such as drip irrigation, rainwater harvesting, and soil moisture monitoring, hemp farmers can reduce their water usage and minimize the impact on local water sources.

Additionally, using cover crops and mulch can help to retain soil moisture and prevent erosion, further conserving water and protecting the environment.

In addition to organic cultivation and water conservation, sustainable hemp farming also involves energy efficiency and waste reduction. By using renewable energy sources such as solar panels and wind turbines, hemp farmers can reduce their reliance on fossil fuels and lower their carbon footprint. Recycling and composting organic waste can also help to minimize the amount of waste generated on the farm, while also providing valuable nutrients back to the soil. These practices not only benefit the environment, but they can also save farmers money in the long run by reducing input costs and increasing efficiency.

Overall, sustainable practices in hemp farming are essential for the long-term success and viability of the hemp industry. By prioritizing organic cultivation, water conservation, energy efficiency, and waste reduction, hemp farmers can help to protect the planet and ensure a healthy future for the hemp industry. As consumers, we can also support sustainable hemp farming by choosing products that are grown and produced in an environmentally-friendly manner. By working together, we can create a more sustainable and prosperous future for hemp farming and the planet as a whole.

Chapter 8

Conclusion

Recap of Key Points

In this subchapter, we will recap the key points covered in "The Complete Guide to Hemp Farming: A Beginner's Handbook" to help reinforce your understanding of the important concepts in hemp farming. Whether you are just starting out or looking to expand your knowledge, these key points will serve as a valuable reference guide for all hemp farmers.

First and foremost, it is crucial to understand the legal landscape surrounding hemp farming. Hemp is a versatile crop that has been legalized at the federal level in the United States under the 2018 Farm Bill. However, it is important to stay informed about any state- specific regulations and licensing requirements to ensure compliance with the law.

Secondly, selecting the right hemp varieties is essential for a successful harvest. Factors such as climate, soil type, and intended use should all be taken into consideration when choosing which hemp strains to cultivate. Additionally, understanding the different types of hemp – such as fiber, grain, and CBD – will help you determine the best fit for your farming operation.

Proper soil preparation and cultivation techniques are also key components of successful hemp farming. Hemp thrives in well-drained, fertile soil with a pH level between 6.0 and 7.5. Implementing sustainable farming practices, such as crop rotation and cover cropping, will help maintain soil health and maximize yields.

When it comes to pest and disease management, prevention is key. Regular scouting and monitoring of your hemp crops can help identify any potential issues early on. Integrated pest management strategies, such as using beneficial insects and natural predators, can help minimize the need for chemical pesticides.

Lastly, harvesting and processing your hemp crop requires careful planning and attention to detail. Timing is crucial when it comes to harvesting hemp for fiber, grain, or CBD production. Proper drying and storage techniques will help maintain the quality of your harvest and ensure a successful end product. By following these key points, you will be well-equipped to navigate the world of hemp farming and achieve success in this dynamic industry.

Resources for Further Learning

In order to truly excel in the world of hemp farming, it is essential to continue learning and expanding your knowledge base. There are a plethora of resources available to help you deepen your understanding of the industry, cultivation techniques, regulations, and best practices. This subchapter, "Resources for Further Learning," will provide you with a curated list of resources that are sure to enhance your expertise in hemp farming.

One of the most valuable resources for further learning in hemp farming is online courses and webinars. Organizations such as Hemp Industry

Daily and the Hemp Industries Association offer a variety of educational opportunities that cover a wide range of topics related to hemp cultivation, processing, and marketing. These courses are often taught by industry experts and can provide you with invaluable insights and practical knowledge that you can apply to your own farming operation.

Another valuable resource for further learning in hemp farming is books and publications. There are many excellent books available that cover a wide range of topics related to hemp cultivation, including soil health, pest management, and harvesting techniques. Some recommended titles include "The Hemp Cookbook" by Marihuana Growers and "Hemp Bound" by Doug Fine. Additionally, industry publications such as Hemp Today and Hemp Magazine are great sources of up-to-date information and insights from industry leaders.

Attending industry conferences and trade shows is another excellent way to further your knowledge in hemp farming. These events provide you with the opportunity to network with other farmers, industry professionals, and suppliers, as well as attend educational sessions and workshops. Some of the top hemp industry conferences include the NoCo Hemp Expo, the Southern Hemp Expo, and the Hemp Industries Association Conference.

Utilizing online forums and community groups is another valuable resource for further learning in hemp farming. Platforms such as Reddit, Facebook, and LinkedIn have dedicated groups for hemp farmers where you can ask questions, share experiences, and connect with other like-minded individuals. These forums are a great way to stay informed about industry trends, regulations, and best practices, as well as seek advice and guidance from experienced farmers.

Lastly, partnering with agricultural extension services and local universities can also be a valuable resource for further learning in hemp farming. These organizations often offer workshops, field days, and research trials specifically tailored to hemp farmers. By leveraging their expertise and resources, you can stay at the forefront of industry developments and gain valuable hands-on experience that can help you improve your farming practices.

Final Thoughts on Hemp Farming

As we wrap up our discussion on hemp farming, it is important to reflect on the potential this industry holds for individuals of all backgrounds. Hemp farming is not only a lucrative business opportunity, but it also has numerous environmental benefits that can contribute to a more sustainable future. By growing hemp, farmers can help reduce carbon emissions, preserve soil health, and promote biodiversity. It truly is a versatile crop that can benefit everyone, from farmers to consumers.

One key takeaway from this handbook is the importance of proper planning and research before diving into hemp farming. Understanding the regulations surrounding hemp cultivation, selecting the right seeds, and implementing effective pest management strategies are all crucial aspects of a successful hemp farming operation. By taking the time to educate yourself and seek guidance from experienced farmers, you can set yourself up for success in this rapidly growing industry.

Another important consideration for those interested in hemp farming is the potential for innovation and diversification. Hemp can be used to produce a wide range of products, from textiles and paper to food and biofuels.

By exploring different avenues for utilizing hemp, farmers can maximize their profits and contribute to the growing popularity of this versatile crop. With the right approach, hemp farming can be a rewarding and sustainable venture for individuals of all skill levels.

It is also worth noting the growing demand for hemp products in various industries, from cosmetics and skincare to construction and automotive. As consumers become more environmentally conscious and seek out sustainable alternatives, the demand for hemp-based products is expected to continue to rise. By getting involved in hemp farming now, you can position yourself to capitalize on this trend and establish yourself as a key player in the industry.

In conclusion, hemp farming offers a wealth of opportunities for individuals looking to enter the agricultural sector or diversify their existing operations. By following the guidance provided in this handbook and staying informed about the latest developments in the industry, you can build a successful and sustainable hemp farming business. Whether you are a seasoned farmer or a newcomer to the field, hemp farming has something to offer everyone. So, take the plunge and explore the possibilities of hemp farming today!

Hemp farming is environmentally friendly

Hemp farming is an environmentally friendly practice due to its sustainability, carbon sequestration, biodegradability, versatility, and soil health benefits. It requires less water and pesticides than traditional crops, while its deep root system improves soil quality and reduces erosion. Additionally, hemp absorbs carbon dioxide and releases oxygen, contributing to the fight against climate change. Its versatility allows for the production of various eco-friendly products, further reducing environmental impact.